The Hacker's Guide to Golf:

The story of golf and the people who play it...badly

Bob Meddles

The Hacker's Guide to Golf:
The Story of Golf and the People Who Play it... Badly

Address all inquiries to Bob Meddles at SlapHappyEnt@gmail.com

Published by
Slap Happy Entertainment
SlapHappyEnt@gmail.com

Copyright © 2014, Bob Meddles

ISBN: 978-1-63452-324-0

Author
Bob Meddles
www.BobMeddles.com

Editing/Proofreading
Merrell Knighten
editors@doublereadediting.com

Illustrations
CABoyer
caboyer49@gmail.com

Interior Design
D G Designs
http://dgdesigns.businesscatalyst.com

Printed in the United States of America
Frist Edition November 2014

To Mom & Dad who have always inspired laughter and without whom I might never have gotten this darn thing done.

TABLE OF CONTENTS

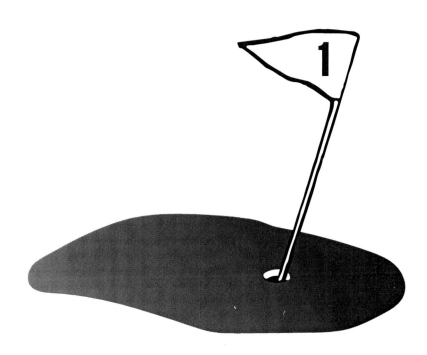

Why Golf?

Why Golf?

I TOOK UP GOLF SOME **25** YEARS AGO SO THAT I WOULD HAVE SOMETHING I could do as I got older and could no longer participate in some of the sports I played earlier in life. In retrospect, I probably should have picked something less frustrating, like learning Mandarin Chinese or working as Adrian Peterson's PR man.

I'd played plenty of other sports over the course of my life, and they had taken their toll on my body. I knew I wouldn't be able to keep playing those same games and still expect to be walking later in life, so golf seemed like the perfect alternative.

Many of my friends and business associates already played the game[1], and I figured it would give me a chance to get outside and enjoy some relatively low-key exercise while still engaging in a competitive activity.

Oh, yeah, and there's a little cart that comes around every so often to bring you beer.

They don't have a beer cart in racquetball, so this seemed like the better choice.

What I didn't know was that while I was a bit of a natural athlete in most endeavors, not great, but capable, that was not the case with golf. And that is simply because there is nothing natural about golf.

---

1 Yet not a single one of them tried to discourage me from taking it up, which makes me wonder what kind of friends they really were.

For example, I tried skiing many years ago, and after a few runs on the beginner's slopes I was headed off to the intermediate slopes later that day, where I enjoyed myself immensely.

Conversely, after taking up golf and playing and practicing for a year, I could hit a driver 300 yards … I just had no idea which window it was going to break when it landed.

In fact, after playing for two years, I ended up leaving my driver in the garage and playing without it in order to *improve my score.* That's right. After two years of practice and play, I was actually less competent than when I first started playing and had zero experience.

Such is the nature of this game. In fact, it was once described by Woodrow Wilson as "An ineffectual attempt to put an elusive ball into an obscure hole with implements ill-adapted to the purpose."

That actually used to be the marketing slogan for golf, but corporate found it wasn't pulling them in the way they had hoped, so they changed it. For a brief while it was *Golf: It beats mowing the lawn* before it was ultimately changed to *Seriously, it will get you out of the house for the better part of a Saturday.*

Golf can be the most exasperating activity you are ever likely to spend hundreds and thousands of dollars on, even when you finally begin to improve, and I am not speaking from personal experience here, just handing down apocryphal accounts, as I have never actually improved.

When you get your handicap down to an 18 and can call yourself a bogey golfer, you only want to drop it to below 10 so you can number yourself among the "single-digit" handicap golfers, and once you get there, you want to cut even more strokes off so you can play in that championship flight at your club. And even then it doesn't end. Check out your club pros or better yet, touring professionals. They get checks with six figures on them on a regular basis, but are they happy?

Okay, the six-figure checks make them kind of happy, and their trophy wives don't hurt, but seriously, these guys seldom crack a smile and will always tell you they think they could have played a little better.

If *they* can't be satisfied, what hope is there for the rest of us? But once you start playing, you will always be chasing that elusive shot or two you left out on the course. It is frustrating in a way no other sport can match.

At this point you may be asking yourself why, if golf is so frustrating, anyone would continue to play.

Did I not mention the beer cart?

Seriously, as maddening as the game can be, it is not without its charms.

There's little that can compare with playing a decent round on an early fall day amid pastoral surroundings, in the company of good friends. Then there's the feeling you get when you hit that one shot exactly as you had planned, and it rolls up to within kick-in distance of the hole, all but guaranteeing you a birdie and a five dollar skin from your playing partner, who normally treats you like his own personal ATM.

Or the experience of battling relentlessly throughout the course of a round, bringing to bear all of your wits and focus and imagination to ultimately card a score you didn't even think was within your grasp, but hence becomes the new milepost by which all efforts will be measured.

Golf offers many benefits, not all of them immediately apparent, but they are there for the player who refuses to give up and learns to weather both the highs and the lows. It is all a matter of perseverance.

As Jack Nicklaus once said, "It takes hundreds of good golf shots to gain confidence, but only one bad one to lose it."

On the other hand, it takes only a couple shots at the nineteenth hole to forget that bad shot, so … carry on … and where's that beer cart?

Driving Obsession

Driving Obsession

Drive for show, putt for dough.

THE AXIOM IS AS OLD AS GOLF. WE AS GOLFERS KNOW IT, WE BELIEVE IT and we live by it. It's a known fact that putting makes up 40% to 55% of the game. It's simple: If you want to improve your game, learn to hit more three-to-six-foot putts. If you do, you'll see your score drop more rapidly than a sand wedge hit into a head-wind.

That is why every free moment we have–and I am speaking only of the male golfer here–you will find us heading to the golf course with a single club in our hand. Once there, we will head for the practice facility and hit dozens, even hundreds of balls with that one club.

And that club is, of course, the driver.

Hey, we don't care what the magazines say about putting, even though we read them all faithfully. And we certainly don't care what the pros say, even though we dress in those same snappy outfits they wear. And we sure as hell aren't going to be intimidated by some stupid little three-foot putt, especially when the rules state that we have the option to reach across the hole with the putter in our off hand, take a cursory swipe at the ball with the back edge of the putter and then score it as if we made it, whether it ever sees the bottom of the jar or not. Hey, look it up. It's right there in the Rules of Golf. I believe it's in section 18.1d or John 3:16 or something like that.

The point is, putting is for those who can't grip it and rip it. Driving is for the real men and it is WHY we play the game.

- We want to whack the ball.
- We want to hammer the pill.
- We want to tag one.
- We want to bust it.
- We want to let the big dog eat!

You let a guy reach the green on a par-four from the tee box just once and it will become the defining moment of his life. Forget about the day he graduated from college or when he got married or even the first time he looked upon his newborn child. That one green, reached so improbably with a single blast from the tee box, will from that point forward become the single most important moment in his life.

It doesn't matter that the ball made the green only because the tees were at the very front of the box on that 310-yard par four. It is of no consequence that the ground was harder than an airport runway, and you can disregard the fact that there was a gale-force wind at his back when he teed up his illegal ball and that one time out of a hundred, caught it on the screws of his 52" graphite-shafted driver with the oversized head and spring-like effect.

None of that matters.

What does matter is that that one moment will become "His Golf Story" until the end of time. Because men do not care about dropping more three-to-six-foot putts. Nope. All we really want is to hit the ball an extra 10 yards off the tee box. Never mind that it won't show up on the scorecard. We don't care. We just want to hear the three other guys in our foursome whistle appreciatively though their teeth as they watch our tee shot fade from sight, leaving us only a wedge to the green where mere mortals would require at least a 7-iron.

We want to savor the click as titanium meets surlyn in a big, explosive wet kiss. We want children to squeal, women to faint and the Strategic Air Command to go on alert each time we launch our tee shots.

And it is of only minor consequence that our attempts to squeeze an extra 10 yards out of our drives may result in our tee shots going 50 yards off line. Fairways are for wimps anyway. Having a ball roll into the rough can actually be a bonus. With a little luck the wayward Titleist may roll onto a tuft of grass, sitting high enough for us to hit our driver one more time. It's a win/win situation.

Now I may have oversimplified a bit here, so let me clear this up.

Not every single guy who has ever swung a golf club wants only to hit the ball an extra 10 yards. Some want to hit it an extra 15 yards.

The fact is, most of us would rather win the long drive contest at our home club than the Nobel Peace Prize. Seriously, you think anybody ever slapped the Dalai Lama on the back and shouted, "You da man"?

I think not.

Hitting the ball long is what brings us out and what keeps us coming back despite those triple-digit scorecards that we conveniently forget to grab from the golf cart.

Now if you'll excuse me, I'm on my way to the pro shop. My new driver with the titanium face and the testosterone-releasing grip has just come in, and I have a date with the driving range.

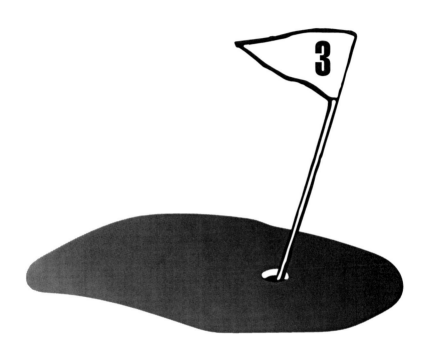

The Golf Swing Explained
Part 1

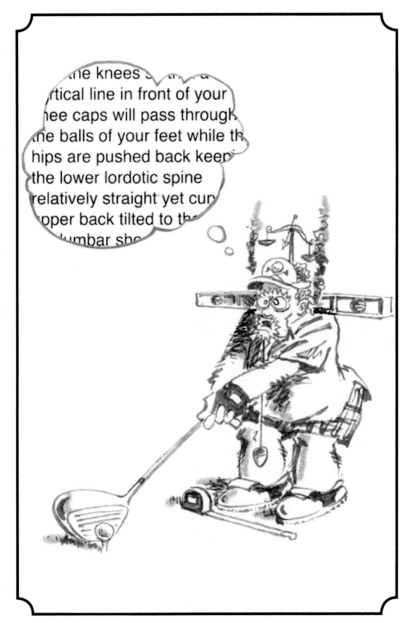

The Golf Swing Explained-Part 1

IN BEN HOGAN'S CLASSIC GOLF INSTRUCTION MANUAL FIVE LESSONS: *The Modern Fundamentals of Golf*, the nine-time majors winner explains that there are four basic parts to the golf swing.

Well, that's not so bad.

Just four parts?

A monkey should be able to deal with just four parts, right?

Of course, there are different theories. Some say there are five parts; others say six. It all comes down to which theory you would like to adopt, and if you start looking at the subparts that make up those 4-6 parts, the number grows a little–to maybe 12 or 347 things you need to concentrate on during the swing.

Whatever the actual number, I think we can all agree that there is kind of a lot to remember in the 1.2 seconds it takes to execute a golf swing, but don't be discouraged. There are several disciplines for achieving the perfect golf swing. In fact, a recent Google search for "golf" and "how to" turned up nearly two billion entries. The same search replacing the words "brain surgery" for golf turned up fewer than 40 million.

So quit whining and start learning … or you could take the easy way out and just become a brain surgeon … quitter!

But you don't have to bother sifting through 1.9 billion possibilities for learning golf. I've boiled them down here to a few hundred words. No thanks needed. Just buy me an island when you cash that first check from a PGA win.

Let's start with:

THE GRIP

The grip is the foundation of the golf swing, and there are a variety of grips that can be successfully employed: Interlocking, overlapping, neutral, strong and weak are some of the most common, but there are others—Babe Ruth's Revenge, the chicken choker, the needy supplicant and the Luke Skywalker, where you grip the club like a light saber and hope the Force will guide your shots.

It won't.

Which grip you choose is a matter of personal preference, but the one thing pretty much everyone agrees on is that no matter what style grip you choose, it should never be overly tight. One axiom states you should grip your club as if you are gripping a live bird. I can't think of a single circumstance wherein I would be gripping a live bird with both hands, but hey, I'm not a professional golfer, so what do I know?

Next up:

STANCE AND POSTURE

This is where you set yourself up to make the perfect golf shot, and it couldn't be simpler. Start from the ground up. Your feet should be about shoulder-width apart. How wide are your shoulders? How would I know?

You brought a tape measure, didn't you?

Now, flex your knees so that a vertical line in front of your kneecap will pass through the balls of your feet. By riveting a pair of plumb bobs to your knees, you will easily be able to test for the correct flex.

You brought plumb bobs, right?

As you bend your knees you will want to push your hips back, much as you would if you were preparing to reach for the soap you dropped in the prison shower … bad example. Let's try something else. One golf instructor stated that when you are in the proper position, you should "feel like a competitive Olympic swimmer" poised to dive into the pool.

You know how that feels, right?

Do that.

Now let's get that spine in the proper position.

You want the lower back relatively straight with a small degree of curvature in the upper back. That's not very clear, so let me try to be a bit more precise by using the language of a professional instructor: You want the lumbar spine to be slightly lordotic, but not so much that it is kyphotic.

Now that we've cleared that up, let's move on to the position of the arms and hands.

Now that you have the correct amount of knee flex, hip bend and spinal alignment, it's a simple matter to get your arms in the proper position. Your arms should be positioned so that a vertical line running from the shoulder will pass through your upper arm in front of the kneecap and through the ball of the foot.

Hope you brought more plumb bobs.

Now you are in position to make the perfect golf swing.

Just kidding.

We've barely scratched the surface of the proper stance and posture. We still need to get your spine tilted slightly to the right, your right shoulder lowered below your left, your head behind the ball and your left hip raised slightly above your right. If you brought a level, and if you didn't I can't imagine how you were planning to play golf, it will be easy to check all of these variables.

Let's not forget how far you should be positioned from the ball. You've still got that tape measure, don't you? Now and only now can you begin the golf swing, wherein you put your right foot in, you take your right foot out you put your right foot back in–wait. That's the hokey-pokey. Don't do that.

We'll get to that shortly.

The important thing is now you have all the basics for the stance and posture that will allow you to hit the perfect golf shot.

Or do you?

To be fair, we just went through no fewer than a dozen distinct elements for getting set up to the ball. That's a lot to remember. The simplest way to check to see if you have put yourself in the right stance and posture is simply by feel.

Does it FEEL right? If it does, you are definitely doing it wrong.

Get those plumb bobs and the level and tape measure back out and get to work, slacker!

You'll know you've got it down when you set up to hit a shot and feel a little like Quasimodo trying to pick up trash along the highway.

Those are the first two elements of the golf swing, and we haven't even begun to swing the club, but don't worry. You've already done ALL of the hard work I'm going to give you in this chapter ... because I'm placing the last two elements of the swing in a separate chapter.

May God have mercy on your soul.

The Golf Swing Explained
Part 2

The Golf Swing Explained-Part 2

Okay. You've got the grip down and you have settled yourself into the correct position from which to execute the perfect golf swing.

The hard work is all done.

Now comes the completely impossible stuff.

THE FIRST PART OF THE SWING

The first part of the swing includes everything from the moment you address the ball through the drawing back of the club to the top of the swing right up until the moment you reverse direction on the downswing to complete your mishit.

It even includes a move called the "waggle." The waggle has been described by many golf pros as a stress-relieving device–a small movement of the hands and wrists to eliminate tension and loosen up the muscles in the hands and arms prior to taking a swing. Usually one or two waggles will accomplish this task; however, professional golfer Sergio Garcia once went through a phase where he would waggle as many as two dozen times before actually beginning his backswing. So engrossed was he with his waggles that It could take more than a half minute from the time he addressed the ball until the time he actually hit the ball. He was so relaxed that other players wanted to kill him.

But the serious business of the first part of the swing begins when you start moving the golf club away from the ball on the backswing. As with every other facet of the golf swing, there are a number of theories on how to accomplish this task, which is convenient, as it also affords you a number of excuses for having failed to accomplish this task.

One of the more popular methods taught for the backswing is the one-piece takeaway. When I first heard about the one-piece takeaway I was thrilled, figuring the fewer moving parts, the better and easier to master. I came to know only later that the term "one-piece takeaway" was a misnomer, like "amicable divorce" or "delicious vegan meal."

Hogan describes the one-piece takeaway by saying "the hands, arms and shoulders move almost simultaneously." It's that "almost" in there that is the tricky part. He later explains in detail that the hands start before the arms and the arms before the shoulders, describing it as a "split-second schedule" that the golfer will "instinctively" acquire.

Ben Hogan is a big fat liar.

Instinct is defined as "a natural or innate impulse, inclination or tendency," and trust me when I tell you, there is **nothing** instinctive or natural about the golf swing. It is a collection of unnatural and potentially dangerous movements strung together in a haphazard manner designed to benefit only that unholy alliance between chiropractors, osteopathic surgeons and big pharmacy.

But let's not waste time arguing as to whether or not Ben Hogan's knickers were constantly ablaze. We have lots more work to do in completing your backswing.

We haven't even begun to talk about the rotation of the hips, the various positions the arms, shoulders and hands must be in during each part of the backswing, and of course, the plane.

We don't have all day here, so just remember this: Your hips should be turned about 45 degrees and your shoulders about 90 degrees. Your left arm should be straight, and your right arm should be at a 90-degree angle with the elbow pointed down. Keep your right knee flexed with your weight on the right side. Your left shoulder should be turned under your chin, your clubface should be parallel to your left forearm, and finally, your left heel should stay flat on the ground.

You're probably wondering how you are supposed to keep track of all these moves your body is making in real time given the .7 seconds it takes to complete the backswing.

Relax.

You don't have to. In fact, Hogan explains that when it comes to your left heel, it really doesn't matter whether it stays on the ground or comes off the ground as much as a quarter or even *a half inch.*

Whew! That's a relief!

THE SECOND PART OF THE SWING

We're coming down the homestretch now.
You've practically got this baby whipped.
Time to bring it all home now and rip that little piece of balata (or balata-like substance) down the fairway.

I know what you're thinking: Bob, my mind is already reeling with the number of swing elements I am trying to remember, and if the second part of the swing is anywhere near as complicated as the first, I might as well head for the bar and begin a preemptive drowning of my sorrows.

I'll be the guy in the corner with the gin and tonic.

Just kidding. I drink beer.

In all seriousness, let me allay your fears. Ben Hogan describes the second part of the swing using just **five simple words** … and more than 6,000 complicated ones.

You'll be addressing such issues as whether you pronated or suppinated your wrists.[2]

How does the plane of your downswing angle compare with that of your backswing angle?

Is your swing path inside-out or outside-in?

And why does Dancing with the Stars keep bringing in people who are clearly by no definition stars?

As complicated as this all might seem, the important thing to remember is that golf is actually a game of mishits (I feel like I should hyphenate that last word, but I'll let you pronounce it any way you want).

If you get frustrated with your swing and can't figure out why you can't get the ball to go where you want it to, take solace in the fact that Ben Hogan, considered by many to have written the definitive text on golf instruction, winner of nine major championships and widely regarded as the greatest striker of the ball to ever grace a course, also said this:

"Reverse every natural instinct and do the opposite of what you are inclined to do and you will come very close to having the perfect golf swing."

How's that first-strike margarita sounding now?

---

2 There are still a number of states with laws on the books that prohibit the suppuration of wrists. Check with your local golf pro or district attorney before proceeding.

As frustrating as this game can be, it can also be a lot of fun and a great way to spend time out of doors with friends. Just try to remember this: The golf swing is like a snowflake; each one is unique and unmatched, and also like a snowflake, as soon as you think you have found the perfect one, it disappears before you can say, "Where's my damn snowflake and why am I all of a sudden shanking my drives into the snack shack?"

Enjoy.

Drive for Show,
Putt for D'oh!

Drive for Show, Putt for D'oh!

PUTTING SHOULD BE THE SIMPLEST PART OF THE GOLF GAME. **A**FTER ALL, once you're on the green you no longer have to concern yourself with trees, bunkers, water hazards or even club selection. Still, it is often the single most confounding part of the game. That smooth, perfectly maintained portion of the course that surrounds the hole has proved to be too much for even some of the best ball strikers in the game.

Volumes have been written on how to become a better putter; countless videos have been created, and teaching professionals make their monthly timeshare payments solely from the cash they pocket attempting to teach the unwashed masses how to find the hole more expeditiously. It's a problem with no easy solution.

Even on days when you find yourself hitting fairways and greens with more frequency than Taylor Swift writing a song about the guy that done her wrong, a balky putter can turn 79s into 89s, 89s into 99s and 99s into "Where the Hell is the beer cart?!"

Whether it's yips, lips or rips, putting problems are as diverse as the golfers who suffer from them. Now, lest you think this essay can help you cure any of those myriad maladies, I should warn you: I cannot fix your problem; I can only diagnose it, pretty much like the guy who works on my car.

After exhaustive research, and by exhaustive research I mean spending countless hours sitting on the patio of my local course's clubhouse, beer in hand, watching golfers practice on the adjacent putting green, I've come to the following conclusion: Bad putters fall into one of four groups:

- The 97-pound Weakling
- Rocket Man
- Johnny Can't Read
- Head Cases

Read on to see if you or a loved one falls into one of these categories.

97-Pound Weakling

The 97-pound weakling doesn't buy into that "never up, never in" maxim. No, he coaxes his ball to the hole with a series of loving taps designed not to mar the surface of the precious orb. He is so afraid of hitting the ball past the hole that instead, he demonstrates

the theory that if you continually halve the distance between your-self and a destination, you will never actually arrive. The 97-pound weakling typically owns cats with names like Mr. Whiskers and lives with his mother.

Rocket Man

Rocket Man's difficulty is the exact opposite of the 97-pound weak-ling's. He hits everything with authority! "Never leave a birdie putt short" is his mantra, and you will hear him utter those exact words right before executing the launch sequence that will rocket his ball 15 feet past the hole, defying the laws of gravity as it passes direct-ly over the center of the cup without ever dipping even minutely.

It is not unusual for Rocket Man to have to yell "fore!" after a lag putt. Rocket Man owns every Arnold Schwarzenegger movie ever made and would sooner starve to death than eat yogurt.

Johnny Can't Read

This group includes those who just can't figure out the subtle and not so subtle nuances of the putting surface, but also includes those who accurately read the green, only to misalign or mishit their putt so that they are offline anyway. Many of these players have a surveyor's eye when it comes to judging distances, but simply have no clue as to where the ball is going once it leaves the flat stick. Drunken lemmings have a better sense of direction. Members of this group often work as air traffic controllers and have to ask for direction to the bathroom … even in their own homes.

Head Cases

This last group has the most serious affliction because it can manifest itself in so many different ways, sometimes changing from one day to the next. One day Head Cases may be dropping everything from inside six feet, even if it took three lag putts to get it to that range. On other days they may be nestling lag putts up so close you could one-hand them in blindfolded. Nevertheless, they *will* find a way to miss that tap in.

Those afflicted with this condition often carry more than one putter, thinking they can solve their putting problems by switching clubs, sometimes in the middle of the round. Some will even change putting styles in the middle of a round or go from right- to left-handed or even adopt a previously untried grip on the assumption that things cannot possibly get worse ... but they will.

As their opponent, you should not discourage this type of behavior; instead you should double the bet. Some people call this callous, but I call it tough love ... as well as sound financial advice.

Head Cases tend to talk to themselves and are frequently featured on the Jerry Springer Show.

Maybe you recognize yourself in one of these groups. Maybe you recognize a friend or playing partner. In any case, you can take heart in knowing that understanding your problem is half the battle, and I hope I have helped you with that. For the other half ... you're on your own.

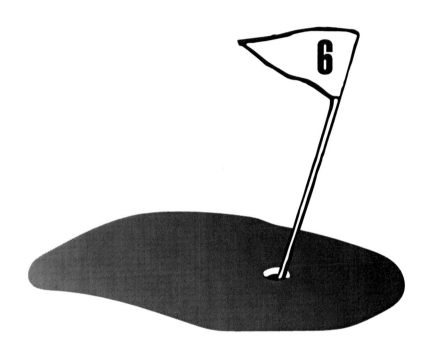

Breaking Up Is
Hard to Do

Breaking Up Is Hard To Do

IT'S NEVER EASY TO SAY GOODBYE. ESPECIALLY TO ONE YOU'VE CARED for and who has cared for you. One who has been there through good times and bad. But there comes a time for honesty. A time when you have to weigh those bad times against the good and ask yourself honestly which way the scales are tipping.

I've recently reached just such a juncture, and it is tearing me apart. I've done the soul searching. I've questioned who should shoulder the blame, but when it comes right down to it, it simply doesn't matter. The only thing that's important is that the time has come for us to call it quits.

I'm bidding farewell to my 60-degree wedge.

She's been with me for years and through countless rounds of golf. You expect relationships to change over time. I mean neither one of us is as young as we used to be. Sure, her face doesn't sparkle the way it did when we first met, but every blemish simply adds more character and makes me love her more. And maybe she doesn't have that same bounce she once had, but that kind of thing doesn't matter to me. What we had went deeper than those superficialities. We had trust and a deep and abiding respect. By God, we had history!

But we've been having trouble communicating of late.

Who am I kidding?

We haven't been on speaking terms for the past six months. At first I didn't think much of it. No one's perfect, so the first time she let me down, I just let it go. That nice soft lob that should have nestled up to the pin turned into a bladed shot into a hazard a good 20 yards over the green.

I didn't say anything, just casually laughed it off. But then it began happening more and more often. I thought maybe she was just looking for a little extra attention. After all, I'd been taking her for granted for years.

I'd make it up to her.

I arranged for a complete makeover. You know how the girls love that kind of stuff. And I went all out. New grip. One of those little leather things that I know she loves. A complete facelift with groove cleaning and head polish to give her back that old sparkle. I even had her loft and lie checked and adjusted. Hey, we all sag a little as time takes its toll. She was good as new. Maybe better. But it didn't matter. Still, she'd have nothing to do with me.

I didn't give up though. I thought maybe the problem was that I simply wasn't spending enough time with her, so I made plans to remedy that. I spent extra time with her at the chipping green. We labored together over soft high shots, spent time on low running chips. I even tried to spice things up with a little blade putting.

Nothing.

But I still wasn't ready to give up. As a last resort, we tried counseling. I found a nice PGA pro who was willing to do couples' therapy. We spent hours with him working on our "problems," but nothing helped.

Maybe it's my fault. Maybe I expected too much of her. I just got so used to running to her every time I got in a little trouble. And she was always there. Getting me out of scrapes I had gotten myself into, through no fault of hers. I came to just assume she would always be there for me through thick (rough) and thin (lies).

But I was wrong.

I'd finally reached my lowest point. I was desperate and as much as I hated to admit it, I started seeking out the company of other wedges behind her back. At first it was no big deal. You know how it goes. You're hanging around the pro shop, just looking around, when it happens. There in the corner, you see her. She's beautiful! And hey, what could it hurt to just introduce yourself?

But from that first moment you meet, something just feels right.

There's electricity.

Then the ever-accommodating club pro invites you to take her out and get to know her a little on the range. No obligation. Just see if you two hit it off. You tell yourself you shouldn't. You tell yourself nothing can ever come of it, but you know even then, it's going to happen. You can't keep your hands off of her. And she'll do anything to please you. Things your old wedge hasn't done in years. High lobs that stop almost before they hit the putting surface. Low runners that check up just short of the hole and then roll ever so enticingly to within inches of the pin, teasing you, tempting you.

Hell, she'll even let you use a cross-hand grip on her.

Oh, she's good.

And she knows how much you want her.

Suddenly you find yourself spending more and more time with her, and before you know it, you're making plans for the future. Maybe a long weekend. Or how about that weeklong trip with the boys?

She'd be nice to have around.

Without even consciously thinking about it, you start working on a plan to get rid of the old ball and chain. Maybe a trip to the pro shop for a new grip where she could conveniently be forgotten. Or maybe the next time the two of you go into a sand trap she doesn't come out. Or maybe, just maybe, she'll have a little accident and solve all your problems. What if you just happened to back over her in the driveway?

Things like that happen every day, right?

What am I thinking?

I can't do that. We've meant too much to each other for too long. She deserves better. Besides, she knows. She has to know. Hell, maybe I want to get caught.

It doesn't matter anymore.

I screw up my courage, prepare for the inevitable scene, but there is no scene. She's actually calm. Says she wants only the best for me and hopes I'll be happy. But there's something not quite right. Like she knows something that I don't. Like she's looking into my future and sees me replaying this same scene over and over again, my contentment only a fleeting thing, always just out of reach.

No.

She's wrong.

This is the real thing. This time it's going to last forever. But just in case, this time, I'm getting a pre-nup...and keeping the receipt.

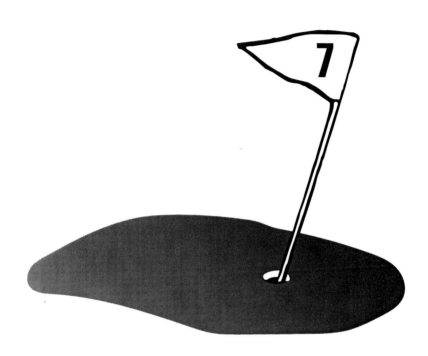

The Lesson
Part 1

The Lesson – Part 1

WHY SHOULD YOU TAKE GOLF LESSONS? AFTER ALL, BUBBA WATSON has never had a lesson in his life, yet he has six PGA tour victories including a win at the Masters.

C'mon.

If a guy named Bubba can advance to the highest level of professional golf without the benefit of lessons or even a real first name, why can't you?

You have to keep in mind, Bubba has spent years creating his swing and countless hours honing it on the driving range, rehearsing that creation over and over until it has become second nature to him; repeatable and solid as railroad steel. And don't even get me started on the staggering number of live chickens that had to be sacrificed to make that swing a reality.

You see, the golf swing is not a natural thing. It was developed by shepherds tending their flocks in Scotland, and you can imagine what kind of unnatural things lonely shepherds are capable of.

Developing a repeatable and effective golf swing on one's own would be akin to learning to do surgery by trial and error. It can be done, but it won't be pretty, and there will be lots of big, ugly scars.

There are just so many moving parts to a golf swing, each dependent on another, that it's a miracle it ever comes together for anyone *but* the touring professional, much less for amateurs out there trying to figure the whole thing out for themselves. I'd have more luck rebuilding a small block Chevy engine blindfolded and without a manual. I guess if I were blindfolded the manual wouldn't be all that helpful anyway, and let's not even get started on the fact that I'm not qualified to top off windshield washer fluid, but you get my drift.

So when is the best time to start taking lessons?

Ideally, if you have never swung a golf club, that is the perfect moment to take lessons: before you have developed any bad habits or misconceptions and before anyone can organize an intervention to keep you from playing golf at all.

You have the opportunity to start things out right.

Think back to other things you've tried for the first time. You were probably awkward and nervous and completely unsure of yourself. Maybe you'd seen some magazines and had a general idea of what goes where, but the finer details were a complete mystery.

How much better might things have gone if I (I mean you) had been instructed by someone[3] who had been around the block. Someone who knew the ropes and could be sure you were doing things right rather than just letting you flail about aimlessly with only a vague idea of what you were trying to accomplish. Certainly you practiced by yourself, but there's nothing like getting out there where all the strokes count and there are no gimmees. ..

Where was I?

Oh yeah, golf lessons.

Once you make the decision to take golf lessons, it's time to select your instructor. This task is not to be taken lightly. You'll be

---

[3] Say, Mrs. Doane, who taught Algebra and wore those really tight sweaters.

spending a lot of time together, often at odds over how things should be done so you want to be sure that the two of you can get past any minor skirmishes or dust ups or assault charges.

The good news is, there are lots of professionals to choose from. Unfortunately, trying to select the right pro blindly can be a tricky proposition. Finding the right golf pro is a little like finding the right therapist. You want someone to whom you can tell everything. Someone who will listen and observe and figure out your quirks and nuances and then gently but steadily set you on the right path. Someone who has access to high quality pharmaceuticals and can take a punch.

The pro, on the other hand, wants someone with a "can-do" attitude and a good line of credit.

I'm kidding.

The "can-do" attitude is optional.

Seriously, the pro is every bit as committed to improving your golf game as you are … just not all at once. There are, after all, speedboats to pay off.

So how does one go about finding the right golf instructor?

If you were engaged in something as trivial as finding the right life partner, you would have dozens of matchmaking websites to help you do that, guaranteeing your success–or so I've been led to believe. But there are are no such sites when trying to pair golf instructor and golf instructee … until now!

With the advent of my brand new website Tee4Two.com, golfers of all abilities will be able to find the instructor who is perfect for them.

Here's how it works.

First, send me $250. This will cover the cost of processing your application, cross-checking it against the hundreds of professional instructors in the database, and of course, gin.

Next, fill out the straight forward application letting us know how much golf you have played, your average score, the areas you are looking to improve in, the best method for peeling hard boiled eggs, and a haiku depicting your level of commitment and enthusiasm. (You can substitute an interpretive dance clip if you are more of a visual communicator).

Your application will then be fed into our high speed supercomputer.[4] Using a sophisticated set of algorithms, proprietary software and a magic eight ball, you will then be matched with the pro who is perfectly suited to help you get the most out of your game-one who has years of experience, a thorough understanding of both the game and the rules of golf, and one who is current in his subscription fees with Tee4Two.com and has no outstanding warrants. The screening process is grueling.

Once you've been matched with your golfing guru, it's time to meet the person with whom you will be spending a great deal of time. But remember, safety first. Be sure to meet the first time at a public place that is well-lit, with lots of people around, like, say a golf course ... you probably could have figured that out for yourself.

You are now ready to embark on a great adventure. It will not be without its challenges, but nothing worth having comes without a great deal of work and persistence ... except maybe winning the lottery. That requires no real effort and is definitely worth having.

Ralph Waldo Emerson once said, "Life is a journey, not a destination," and the same can be said about golf: It is the pursuit of the unattainable that gives us so much pleasure ... as well as ulcers.

---

4 Actually, it's a Commodore 64, but it still runs remarkably well ... or remarkably, it still runs, anywho ....

In any event, including match play, enjoy the journey, and if you take nothing else from this chapter, please remember this:

Tee4Two.com is not responsible for losses or damages consequential or incidental arising from or relating to the conduct of either party involved. Tee4Two.com shall be held blameless in all civil and criminal matters, and all fees are non-refundable.

Now if you could just initial that here, that would be great.

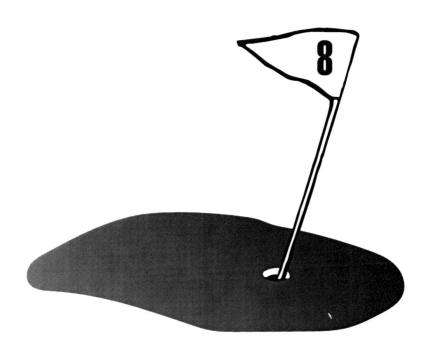

The Lesson
Part 2

The Lesson - Part 2

C ONGRATULATIONS. YOU'VE SELECTED YOUR TEACHING PROFESSIONAL and are now ready to embark on an adventure that will lead to a better swing, more knowledge of the game, lower scores and more fun on the course, not to mention whiter teeth, hair re-growth and an improved sex drive.

The first thing you'll want to do is sit down with your teaching pro-fessional–let's call him Chip–and identify key areas you want to fo-cus on while setting some specific goals you'd like to achieve. You can then go about putting together a practice plan that will ensure you will achieve those goals while simultaneously neglecting your work, family and health.

Hey. Nobody said this was going to be easy.

Chip will likely want to start by adjusting a few things that are just a *bit* off and will get in the way of further instruction if not corrected. You can't build a structurally sound house without a solid founda-tion, and the foundation to your game is every bit as crucial. Chip will likely just "tweak" a few things like grip, stance, positioning, posture, alignment, sideburn length, religious affiliation, hair color and dialect. It shouldn't take more than two or three months to get these squared away, and in no time at all you'll be ready to move forward … or take up tennis.

It could go either way.

One of the most efficient ways to identify the areas where you need work is by video recording your swing. This will allow you to see where the problem areas lie and will afford Chip and his colleagues hours of amusement as they "review" your swing and identify things you should do in order to have a more enjoyable experience–such as taking up tennis.

Just kidding. Even if your swing has been likened to an "arthritic zombie trying to orchestrate Beethoven's Ninth Symphony," Chip will come up with a plan specifically tailored to your needs. There is not a golf swing in the world, no matter how fundamentally flawed, that cannot be transformed into a consistent, repeatable thing of beauty … discounting, of course, Charles Barkley's "swing," which no one should ever look directly at. If you must view his swing due to an all-consuming curiosity or the loss of a bet, use welder's goggles or view it indirectly through the reflected image in a mirror swabbed generously with Vaseline.

Once you've identified the areas where you need work, it's time to get down to it. Rest assured, your teaching professional has worked with hundreds of golfers with every possible swing flaw. He has seen it all, and nothing you bring to the tee will surprise him. Armed with a myriad of teaching techniques, drills and a Xanax prescription, he can help even the most untalented player become a slightly less untalented player.

Be forewarned, your teaching professional may ask you to do some drills that seem strange or odd or even criminally insane. Don't worry. Your pro knows what he is doing, so if he has you swing with only one hand or putt with your eyes closed or provide him with your social security number and ATM PIN, rest assured that he is focused only on improving your game as expeditiously as possible … and funding his annual trip to the Masters.

One of the most common problems high-handicap golfers experience is the outside-in swing. This is when your club starts outside the intended swing plane and then gets pulled inside that plane.

This flawed swing plane causes a number of problems, including sliced shots, pulls, decreased distance, gingivitis, low testosterone levels and jogger's nipple.

On the plus side, getting rid of an outside-in swing couldn't be easier. A few simple drills, a session or two on the range, and a couple of hours with an exorcist, and you'll be hitting the ball long and straight in no time. Just kidding. An outside-in swing is completely incurable and will haunt you all of your days until you give up golf all together or resign yourself to aiming 60 yards left and watching your tee shots travel in an arc that resembles a particularly warped banana or a misshapen horseshoe.[5]

But all the lessons in the world won't do you any good without practice. Remember, you are trying to build a consistent, repeatable swing, and repetition is the only way that is going to happen. As they say, practice makes perfect.

They also say a bird in the hand is worth two in the bush, but take it from someone who has held a bird in his hand … always carry hand sanitizer.

But seriously, get out there and practice.

Practice. Practice. Practice.

If it happens that your consistency comes in the form of shanked approach shots that rocket off the hosel of your club into adjacent fairways threatening the lives of other players on the course, well, technically that's still consistency.

Above all, don't get discouraged.

Remember the story of Abraham Lincoln: Born into poverty, Lincoln never let failure stop him from trying again. His first attempt at

---

5 At this time there is no cure for the outside-in swing, but with your generous donations we will continue the research until we have found that cure or run out of beer. CUE SARA MCGLAUGHLIN.

running for elected office ended in failure, as did his second and third and fourth and fifth and sixth and …. Jeez, why didn't this guy just hang it up? I mean, there's determination, and then there's just pig-headedness.

The point is, through perseverance and dogged determination, he eventually won an election and went on to become a successful pocket change model.[6]

Finally, the sign of a true champion is the ability to get back up after a fall, dust oneself off and try again … as many times as is necessary. Even if you suffer countless failures, a plethora of defeats, mountains of frustrations and person after person constantly telling you that you will never be a good golfer–well, there's always tennis.

---

6 In accordance with full disclosure, his golf swing looked like a teenage girl trying desperately to shoo away a swarm of moths, but his persistence when it came to running for office cannot be questioned.

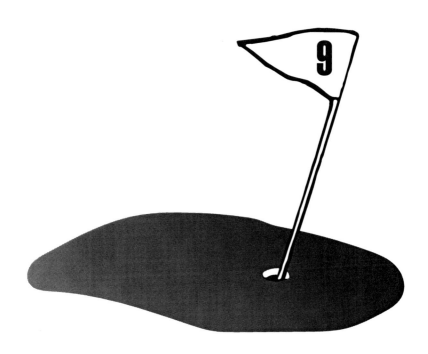

The Right Tool
for the Job

The Right Tool for the Job

ACCORDING TO SOME STATISTICS I JUST MADE UP, EVERY YEAR GOLFERS spend more than $879 million on equipment and devices designed to lower their scores. The bulk of this money was spent by golfers like myself, and by that I mean golfers who cannot count our handicaps without removing our shoes and possibly the spikes of at least one other member of our foursome. Oddly enough, single-digit handicap golfers tend to spend their share of disposable income geared to golf improvement on things like state-of-the-art balls, custom-fitted clubs and, get this, lessons.

Suckers.

Why would you spend your hard-earned money and your hard-to-come-by time on lessons and practice when the golf stores are awash in gadgets that can make you a better golfer without any real effort on your part?

I don't get it.

Literally hundreds of items out there guarantee to improve your game immediately, and if you think I am going to forego that kind of instant gratification in favor of hard work and personal sacrifice, well, you have another think coming.

Watch any of those infomercials that follow a tournament that ended sooner than expected, and you'll see how easy it can be. You know the ones I'm talking about. Those half-hour "documen-

taries" that offer us the chance to straighten our drives, get out
of the sand more expeditiously, and/or drop more putts simply by
purchasing the gadget du jour for four low payments of just $39.95
(and if you act now, we'll make the first payment for you and throw
in this lovely tee cozy at no additional charge).

Look: Deep down, we know we can't really suddenly start hitting
300-yard drives just because we are using a club made from a
petrified giraffe femur epoxied to a vulcanized cantaloupe, but the
siren call of the long ball is simply too much to resist. It's not really
our fault, mostly because nothing in society today is anyone's fault
if you're willing to look for a reason. We're just another segment of
the population looking for a quick fix to a long-term problem.

We're a "lose 10 pounds a week, make $50,000 a month from
home, eat three pounds of bacon and ice cream while lowering
your cholesterol" society. We want to believe in that "no pain/big
gain" theory so badly that we don't care how improbable the claim
is, we just want what we want, and we want it now.

I should know.

Why, you can't swing an articulated driver with built-in feedback
receptors and a molded grip over your head in my house without
banging it into one training device or another. I've got weighted
clubs, clubs that bend in the middle, clubs with laser lights coming
out of either end, clubs with sliding grips, long clubs, short clubs,
practice mats, alignment hats, stance aligners, distance diviners
and more putter training devices than you can swing a flat stick at.

And while I was looking over this massive inventory of training
aids, it occurred to me that I was lured into buying each one of
these devices with a guarantee, a guarantee, mind you, that they
would lower my score from two to six strokes. And they said it right
there on TV, so it has to be true.

I now have a plan.

I am going into seclusion for the next 30 days. During my forced hiatus, I will be practicing with each one of these magical talismans. By the time I emerge in one month, I will be the ultimate golfing machine. The cumulative effect of all this golf gadgetry will no doubt transform me from the hack that my golf buddies have come to know and love into a lean, mean birdie-making machine. My average score should be about 56, and my metamorphosis will be complete when I bankrupt each and every member of my foursome.

I don't know why I didn't think of this before.

Oh, they all laughed at me when I purchased these items, one after another, seeking the perfect swing and my rightful place among the scratch golfers of the world, but no more. It's my time to shine.

Now, if someone will help me fasten my Peter Jacobson Swing Jacket and super glue this titanium aiming rod to my forehead, I will get down to work.

Die Sandbagger, Die!

Die Sandbagger, Die!

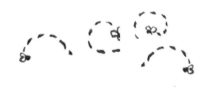

Sandbagger: One who artificially inflates his or her handicap in order to gain a competitive advantage. See also: Scumbag

MANY PEOPLE PLAY GOLF MORE FOR THE CAMARADERIE THAN FOR THE game itself. The chance to spend time with friends is just one of the many reasons to partake in a game that can otherwise be an exercise in frustration.

But maybe you are not one of those people. Maybe you look at golf as a way to get away from others and are annoyed by the fact your solace is impinged upon by the three other players in your group. Maybe you are looking for solitude and respite from the demands of associates and other acquaintances. In fact, maybe you simply have too many friends and are looking for a way to thin the herd, so to speak.

If you find this to be true, might I suggest the ancient art of sand-bagging as a means to that end?

Trust me, becoming a sandbagger will allow you to cull your overcrowded Christmas card list more quickly than if you were to become an Amway agent. Carriers of the Swine Flu are more wel-come in a foursome. The Unabomber has a longer list of people willing to bail him out of jail than the sandbagger.

In point of fact, no other pursuit can so quickly turn friends into sworn enemies as sandbagging. Serial killers and yes, even telemarketers get more respect than sandbaggers and for good reason: While serial killers may be able to point to a life-changing event beyond their control somewhere in their past that steered them down their wayward path, eliciting a modicum of sympathy and understanding if not compassion, sandbaggers are just, well, jerks.

These individuals have bartered their self-respect for a few paltry coins. They have traded their conscience for mere lucre. Yes, they have sold their very soul for nothing more than pro shop payola worth half the value of real dollars and three times that of their character, if they had any. Sandbaggers are the lowest life form on the planet. They possess all the charm of a sexually transmitted disease and are harder to get rid of. And the very worst thing about sandbaggers is that they will spend every waking moment they are not using their puffed-up handicap to rifle through your wallet, trying to convince you they are NOT sandbaggers.

With a handicap system that rivals the IRS tax code in complexity, these remorseless bottom-feeders have elevated the manipulation of that system to an art form, swimming the murky handicap waters with the agility of bottlenose dolphins–lying, cheating, scum-sucking dolphins.

You know the guy I'm talking about; he consistently stripes drive after drive 300 yards down the center of the fairway when there is sufficient coinage on the line, but immediately begins snap hooking his 8-iron into adjacent fairways as soon as he's got you three down with two to play. Magically, the putter that has not failed him from inside 15 feet becomes balky, and he has trouble getting his lags halfway to the hole. And that "once-in-a-lifetime, can't-believe-it-happened" 68 that he shot last week somehow never got reported, leaving his tidy little 19-handicap intact.

Stalkers have more redeeming social value.

Which brings us to the question, "What can be done about this blight on the golf community?"

I have a few suggestions.

THE SCARLET LETTER OPTION

Sandbaggers should be branded with a scarlet "S" on their foreheads. Not only because it would make identification much easier, but also because it would hurt like hell!

REHAB

Perhaps we could open a clinic for sandbaggers; a rehab facility where sandbaggers could work through their issues and discover what caused them to become sandbaggers in the first place. A place where these lying, cheating, miserable excuses for human beings could be nurtured and shown the error of their ways. Of course, once they have completed their rehab, they would still be branded with that scarlet "S" on their forehead, but they'd get a cookie and a hug afterward.

SANDBAGGERS ANONYMOUS

How about a 12-step program? There's a nice drop off behind the 12th hole at Pebble Beach that falls into the ocean. They could start, say, 11 steps from there.

Actually, the only true cure and fair penalty for sandbaggers is to make them play with other sandbaggers. It would be like an elevator full of pickpockets.

I used to think that there was no hope for sandbaggers. I believed them to be beyond salvation and simply something to be graciously endured, like your mother-in-law's dried-up pot roast or the Ebola virus, but then I found hope–a tiny ray of hope, most certainly, but hope nonetheless. That hope was born from the tale of one sandbagger whose life was changed forever through the caring efforts of those he had fleeced one too many times. In the hope that other sandbaggers may someday be persuaded to change their evil ways and come to the light, I offer this story of redemption.

This particular sandbagger was notorious for his sleazy handicap augmentation tactics. He'd happily pad his scores during casual rounds and even a few of the lesser tournaments to be sure he could win our club championship, taking advantage of those he called friends and treating them like his own personal petty cash fund. And though he considered them friends, they looked upon him much as one would a cancerous tumor or festering open sore.

One particular day when a big money game was scheduled, the sandbagger in question "miraculously" shot well below his handicap, taking the lion's share of the bets without so much as offering to buy a single drink after the round, as is customary within our group.

But did we get mad?

No.

Did we report him to the handicap chairman?

No.

We paid off our bets, like gentlemen. And then, like gentlemen, we stripped him naked, bound him hand and foot with duct tape and tossed him in the lake behind the 13th green, where to this day, crawdads still feast on his flesh.

See, happy endings do happen.

Language of Golf
Part 1

Language of Golf – Part 1

GOLF HAS BEEN PLAYED FOR HUNDREDS OF YEARS, AND OVER THE course of that time, a language unique to the sport has evolved, much of which should not be repeated in mixed company. But much of it is also beautiful and concisely descriptive.

Many of the terms commonplace to the avid golfer are a mystery to those just taking up the game, so in an effort to help those who are not fluent in golfspeak, I offer the following lexicon designed to help you understand the basics of the terms used to describe this ancient and hallowed game.

THE SWING

- BACKSWING–The motion which takes the club away from the ball up to and including the point at the top of the swing when you hesitate and begin second-guessing your strategy and drastically changing your swing thought.

- DOWNSWING–The swing forward from the top of the backswing until the moment the ball is mishit.

- FOLLOW THROUGH–The follow through is everything that occurs after ball impact and through the point where your body completes the swing. Many pros like to see what they call the "reverse C" at the end of golf swing. This is where a player's body, from feet through the legs and torso and all the way through the hands and even including the club itself, form a backwards "C" shape. It is a graceful finish that should be held while admiring your best shots.

NOTE: It should not be held while admiring less-than-perfect shots including missed drives (SEE: Whiff), shanked approach shots (SEE: Damnit!!) and certainly not on thinned shots driven through car windows (SEE: Your insurance agent).

THE SHOTS

· DRIVE–The first shot on any hole, hit from the tee box.

· APPROACH–Shots which are meant to hit the green are deemed approach shots. On a par four, this will typically be your second shot while on a par five, it may be your third. The number of approach shots one can have on any given hole is defined only by your skill. Better players may get only a single approach shot on a given hole, but for those of us who like to "sneak up" on a hole, there can be any number of thinned shots, chili dips, skulls, chunks, dribblers, yanks, jerks, quackers, and whiffs amassed before a player actually navigates the territory between tee and green.

· PUSH–A push results from an inside-out swing with the ball traveling left to right (for a right-handed golfer).

· FADE–This describes a shot that move in an arc, slightly left to right (for a right-handed golfer). Properly struck, a skilled player can use this shot to skirt trees or other obstacles that are directly between him and his target.

· SLICE–This is a more pronounced example of the fade, normally employed by less skilled players at random and unexpected points throughout the round. While it can be accounted for and adjusted to, it is seldom if ever played purposefully and has a habit of finding trees, water and out-of-bounds markers more surely than a Kardashian can locate a camera.

- F*&%ING BANANA–This is the bastard son of the slice and given the perfect storm of conditions (wind, open stance, outside-in swing path and bad haircut) can theoretically come all the way back around and hit the player who struck the ball in the temple, killing him. Most players who hit this type of shot pray for that kind of quick and merciful release.

- PULL–A pull results from an outside-in swing and travels right to left (for a right-handed golfer).

- DRAW–A draw is a shot that travels in an arc from right to left. Typically a draw has more roll on it than a fade and thus is favored by many players.

- HOOK–A hook (like a slice) is a more pronounced draw. It starts right and then unerringly moves left while the player who just hit the shot begs (ineffectually) for it to stop.

- SNAP HOOK[7]–A snap hook is basically a f$%#ing banana as seen through a mirror. Snap hooks are the leading cause of irritable bowel syndrome and have contributed greatly to the uptick in prescription pain killer abuse.

- BITE–A ball with spin on it when it hits the green is said to "bite." The backspin on the ball causes it to stop quickly and even reverse its direction. Most commonly this occurs when the ball is online with the hole and its continuing to roll forward would result in a holed shot or tap in. It is just as likely to happen when a player has barely cleared the lake that his ball is about to spin back into.

- SHANK–Also known as a lateral, hosel rocket or "S" word. A shanked shot is one in which the ball is contacted by the hosel (the part of the club that connects the blade to the shaft) rather than the club face. The resultant shot can go anywhere and is

---

7 Did you know that Eskimos have more than two dozen words for snow? Coincidentally, there are more than three dozen colorful terms for the snap hook. None of them are fit for publication in this book.

particularly embarrassing for the "shanker.[8]" A single shanked shot is not uncommon and nothing to worry about; however, repeated shanking is like an infectious disease akin to Herpes or Bieber Fever: painful to live with and impossible to explain to your friends.

- WHIFF—This is a swing in which the club never makes contact with the ball. It is nothing to be embarrassed about and it happens to everyone; now go over there and that nice lady will give you a cookie and a hug.

MISCELLANEOUS STUFF

- FISO—A colorful acronym used to describe one's situation following a disappointing shot, noting that you are still the furthest from the hole. "Fudge (or some similar expletive), I'm Still Out."

- PBFU—Post Birdie F%@k Up. The inevitable triple bogey that is waiting for you following a birdie.

- GIMMEE—A putt that is so short it is "given" to one's competitor without him having to make the putt, despite the fact that the son of a bitch didn't give you that two-footer on the last hole that you clearly would have made if you had not casually backhanded it toward the hole—and while we're at it, he hasn't bought a round of drinks all day, and that umbrella with the putter head handle he carries should really be considered a 15th club, meaning he lost that hole anyway. I'm going to have a talk with the handicap chairman after this round.

- SWEET SPOT—Mythical area purported to be in the center of a club face (SEE ALSO: Yeti, Loch Ness Monster and g-spot).

- THE TIPS—The tees from which single-digit handicap golfers should play and also the tees from which the guys playing in front of you who have never broken 100 will be playing.

---

8 Not to be confused with "chancre," a syphilitic lesion that while more painful, is less embarrassing and easier to get rid of.

- PLUMB BOB–Holding the putter by the handle and letting the club head dangle while assessing the line of approach to determine how badly you will miss your putt.

The entirety of golf terminology cannot possibly be included in a single chapter of this book, partly because I like to keep the chapters short so you don't nod off and also because I need 18 chapters for this book, and by splitting this essay into two separate parts, I have one less chapter idea I have to come up with, but it's mostly for your benefit … mostly.

Language of Golf
Part 2

Language of Golf - Part 2

THE PLAYERS

- SCRATCH GOLFER—A golfer with a very low handicap or none at all. These are the players who are constantly shooting within a few strokes of par, reminding you just how awful you really are.

- BOGEY GOLFER—A Bogey Golfer is generally considered to be a player who has a handicap within two or three strokes of an 18 handicap.

- HACKER—A hacker is a golfer who strives for mediocrity. We have come to terms with the fact that we will never be scratch golfers and happily (or not so happily) will spend our days dwelling in the land of bogies, double bogies and "others." Upon hearing the ubiquitous "I'd rather be lucky than good," we only wish we had an option.

Never forget, however, that according to one source, the average handicap for all male golfers is 16.1, which means that more than half of ALL golfers are hackers.

So wear that mantle proudly as you make that third attempt to get out of the sand, stride with unwarranted self-satisfaction from the green where you just four-putted, and hold your head high as you turn in that card sporting a three-digit total!

And always remember the Hacker's Creed:

EGO venit, EGO saw, EGO lubricus unus in silva.

- *TRANSLATION: I came, I saw, I sliced one into the woods.*

- SANDBAGGER–A despicable individual for whom money and recognition mean more than integrity and honor. SEE ALSO: Kardashian

SCORING TERMS

- HANDICAP–A system that allows players of various abilities to compete equitably. It uses past scores, importance of the round, course rating and slope, the phases of the moon, sunspot activity, and phrenology to arrive at a number used to adjust your gross score. That number will either be not nearly enough (if it is *your* handicap) or "What the Hell do you *mean,* you're a 19?" (if it is your opponent's).

- ESC–Equitable Stroke Control. This is a system designed to keep handicaps in line so that sandbaggers (AKA: cheating jerks) don't artificially inflate their handicaps during casual rounds, only to exploit the inflated handicap during tournaments and money games. Laudable as the idea is, sandbaggers, who have the scruples of reality TV producers, cannot so easily be dissuaded[9].
- (See the chapter titled "Die Sandbagger, Die!" for more information.

- PAR–Each hole is assigned a "par" score, which is the score an accomplished player is likely to make on that hole.

- BIRDIE–Scoring one stroke less than par for any given hole. Also known, by those of us in the brotherhood of hackery, as a damn miracle.

9 And believe me, if we could dissuade those bastards, their suede would be long gone.

- EAGLE–Legend has it that there are those who can hole a ball in two strokes less than par. This feat is called an eagle.

- DOUBLE EAGLE or ALBATROSS–This is just some made-up bullshit!

- ACE–A hole in one. This is such a rare and momentous feat that should you ever be lucky enough to accomplish it, you will have the unique privilege of taking out a second mortgage on your home so that you can buy drinks for everyone at the bar after the round, whether you have ever met them or not.

- IMPORTANT NOTE: If you are ever lucky enough to card an ace, be sure that before you tee it up for the next hole, you step back and ask loudly enough for all to hear, "Did anyone beat a one?" Yes. It's obnoxious, but you may never get this opportunity again, so be sure to bask in it.

- BOGEY–Scoring one over par. Also the term your opponent will add "nice" to, after you miss a three-footer for par and he wins the hole.

- DOUBLE BOGEY–Scoring two over par.

- TRIPLE BOGEY–And the beat goes on.

- SNOWMAN–An eight. A go&$%##med eight!

- STORY HOLE–Any hole on which you card a double-digit score. As in: "What did you score on seven?" "Let me tell you about seven. Once upon a time…."

MISCELLANEOUS GOLF TERMS

- OUT OF BOUNDS–Also referred to as OB, OBIE WAN KANO-BIE and OFF THE RESERVATION. Hitting out of bounds results in one of the most severe penalties in golf in that not only does one incur a one-stroke penalty, but also has to return to where the last ball was struck to re-hit from that same spot. The player who went OB has the added pleasure of enduring the WALK OF SHAME, as he returns to that spot. There he will find the group of golfers that have already been waiting for him to move along so they can continue play, thus their mood may be less than convivial. Thankfully, golfers are a very empathetic group who, noting your pain and embarrassment, will try to soften the blow with words of encouragement like, "You'll get 'em this time," or "This is tough hole," or "Does your husband play too?"

*   PROVISIONAL—A provisional ball is played when a player fears his ball may have gone out of bounds or be lost. By hitting a second ball, time can be saved if the first ball is in fact lost or out of bounds. Before playing such a ball, the player MUST declare the ball as provisional. To do this, the player must close his eyes, spin around three times while singing "I'm a Little Teacup." No. Really. That's what you have to do.

*   PRESS—A bet that allows you to double your losses when things aren't going your way, but you are certain that is about to change.

*   BALLWASHER—Device usually located near the tee box on holes that allows players to rid their balls of sand, grass stains, mud, bad JuJu, and gypsy curses.

*   SCRAMBLE—A tournament format that teams four players to record a single score … or your pace to the port-a-let after consuming a questionable hot dog at the snack shack on the 9th hole.

*   SHOTGUN—A tournament that allows every member of that event to start on various holes at a particular time, allowing the entire group to finish at the same time. Usually about six and a half hours after you start.

• THIN SHOT–A shot that was hit with the front edge of the club in the middle of the ball. Such shots will almost always be hit low and fast and travel much further than intended. This mishit most commonly occurs if there is a plate glass window behind the green you are hitting to.

• FAT SHOT–The opposite of a thin shot, this shot results from taking too much turf, resulting in a divot or beaver pelt. Also known as hitting the big ball first, fat shots fall far short of their intended mark and almost always occur after you have caused your entire group to wait five minutes so you wouldn't "hit any-one on the green."

• LAYUP–What you tell the others in your foursome you were doing when the 230-yard approach shot you had intended to be pin high ends up 100 yards short of the green.

• THIN LIE–A ball resting on little or no grass, or a bad fabrica-tion to explain how the ball everyone saw go into the creek, somehow miraculously fought its way back out and ended up on the green.

While We're Young!

While We're Young!

THERE IS NOTHING QUITE SO PLEASANT AS A MORNING SPENT ON THE golf course… unless that morning turns into an afternoon.

Transforming a great round of golf into a torturous marathon that tests not only endurance, but also the ability to control otherwise latent homicidal tendencies, is as simple as one group of players adding an extra three minutes to every hole they play. A four-hour round quickly (or rather, slowly) becomes a five-hour round, not just for them, but also *for every group playing behind them.*

Slow play is the bane of golf, and much of the blame for that slow play can be placed squarely at the metal-spiked shoes of professional golfers. The guys on TV play like they are headed for their own execution and are delaying that fate by every means possible.

And those who are supposed to monitor such things apparently can't be bothered.

No serious penalty for slow play has been issued to a pro golfer in decades, so it should come as no surprise that the American golfing public believes that is the way the game is to be played.

I say poppycock!

But only because I can't say what I really want to say … which is BULLSHIT!!

I guess I can say it.

While the PGA should penalize slow play according to their own rules, thus speeding play and making it more enjoyable to both play and watch, history says they will not. It's up to others to convince the amateur player that while Ben Crane playing a round of golf might resemble a sloth swimming through tree sap, that doesn't mean he should too.

Speeding up play is easy. In fact, one simple guideline, if adopted by everyone playing golf, would result in speedier, more enjoyable rounds for everyone who ever picked up a niblick.

Here it is: KEEP UP WITH THE GROUP AHEAD OF YOU.

That's it.

It truly is that simple.

Because it is not about staying ahead of the group behind you. You will ALWAYS be ahead of the group behind you. That is not the point.

It's like driving down the interstate in the left lane at 45 miles per hour. In both cases you are ahead of the group behind you … and in both cases the group behind you wants to kill you!

Your job is to keep up with the group ahead of you.

But what if the group ahead of you is slow? That falls into the category of "Not your problem."

As long as you are keeping up with that group in front of you, you are doing all that is expected of you. If play is still slow, it is up to the group in front of you to speed up and up to the course officials to see that they do. Those guys getting free golf to be marshals aren't there just to do shade analysis: They are there, at least in theory, to maintain pace of play.

But maybe you don't want to speed up play.

Maybe you think the perfect round of golf should be six-and-a-half hours long. Maybe you think it should be less about the golf and more about the pleasant walk that you are not about to have spoiled. Maybe you are from an alien planet and subsist on the white-hot hatred of those around you.

Well, if that's the case and you are hell bent on seeing just how long you can make a round of golf last and/or how close you can come to being brutally assaulted by people in plaid slacks that you have never met before, by all means, carry on.

And if that is in fact your goal, allow me to offer a few tips that should aid you in that endeavor, making you the focal point for loathing and contempt for as long as you live … which might well be a shorter span than you think.

1 - Always play from the tips.
Real men play from the tips. Even real men who sport 30-plus handicaps. Besides, playing from all the way back gives you nicely groomed layup areas, also known as the forward tees.

2 - Buy the most expensive balls you can find. Even if you regularly shoot 120, the extra spin and control around the greens will be handy when you blade that baby into the creek. And never forget how much you spent on those balls. If you lose one in the woods, track it down with the vigor of a bloodhound pursuing an escaped axe murderer. The rules may say you have only five minutes to search for a lost ball, and common courtesy would dictate an even shorter search, but when you're playing Bazooka Elites at eight bucks a pop, well, just ignore those people behind you shaking their fists.

3 - Never select the club you are going to use until everyone in your foursome has already played. Sure, you've been standing there by your ball while everyone else has hit their shots, but don't pull that stick from your bag until you have a full audience, thus ensuring they will enjoy every bit of the theater that is your 65-yard chili-dipped approach shot.

4 - When assessing a shot, determine the yardage exactly. And be meticulous.

Sure, the sprinkler head may say 175 yards, and the GPS on the cart could agree. Even your personal range finder might fall into lockstep, but nothing gives you the confidence of knowing you have the precise yardage like walking it off yourself, twice if need be. You know that old adage, "Measure twice, get hit in the head by an 'errant' approach shot for doing so."

But seriously, even if you don't know from one shot to the next if your seven-iron is going 120 yards or 170 yards, don't let that stop you from getting a precise measurement of yardage. Knowing whether you are about to mishit a 120-yard shot or a 121-yard shot can give you a confidence that will radiate from you and make those you are playing with think, "Man, this guy is really a jerk."

5 - Never underestimate the importance of a pre-shot routine and let nothing interrupt that routine. This can be crucial to your success, so if your pre-mishit ritual is in anyway disturbed, back off and start from scratch. For instance, your pre-shot routine might go something like this:

When it is your turn to play, step to the ball, address it (insert Ed Norton joke here if you were born before 1964) step back, take a few practice swings, consult your smartphone for a tutorial on how Phil Mickelson would play this shot, adjust your chakras, check the wind, reshoot the yardage, get a sip of water, lather, rinse, repeat.

After all of that, and only after all of that, are you ready to … hey, is that a woodpecker?

Start over.

6 - Never carry an extra ball in your pocket. It will ruin the line of those picnic tablecloth-inspired slacks you're sporting. Besides, if you lose a ball and need another, you can just walk back to your cart and get one. One, not two. And don't worry about that group behind you. You're actually doing them a favor by giving them time to work on their alibis.

7 - When putting, be sure to circle the entire green, twice if necessary. Look for any nuance that might affect that two-footer you're about to hit. Take into account the break of the green, which way the grain of the grass is oriented, wind, sunspot activity, rotation of the earth, recent fortune cookie advice and astrological influences. But be sure to wait until everyone else has putted before beginning this regimen.

Remember, it's all about you.

8 - Play everything out to the bitter end. I don't care if you are playing match play and your opponent has just jarred his par putt while you are lining up your 13th shot out of the bunker. Play every shot like it's your last … because depending on the concealed carry laws in the state where you are playing, it just might be.

The Rules of Golf

The Rules of Golf

Let your conscience be your guide … but carry a rulebook anyway.

GOLFERS SPEND HOURS HONING THEIR GAME. IT'S NOT UNUSUAL FOR A player to spend his lunch break hitting balls at the range, and it's fairly common to find that those same individuals have some sort of makeshift practice hole in their living rooms so they can work on their putting. Few would find it remarkable that golfers will forego watching the most recent installment of "Survivor XIII: Stranded in Duluth" in order to review a tape of "Golf My Way" for the 167th time. But there is one segment of the game that is often neglected even though it deserves every bit as much attention as driving, chipping or putting. That part of the game is, of course, being able to lie about one's handicap with a straight face.

Just kidding.

Actually, it is a review of the rules. Knowing the rules of golf, or should I say THE RULES OF GOLF, is an aspect of the game which is often neglected, but important on so many levels. Knowing the rules of golf can enhance your enjoyment of the game, save you strokes, and even improve your peristaltic health. Why, without rules, we'd have anarchy, or even worse, professional wrestling.

Yet as important as golf rules are, not everyone who plays the game knows them as well as he or she should. There is good reason for that, that reason being that the Rules of Golf were written by drunken orangutans or possibly IRS tax accountants.

I cite the following example:

Rule 19-1 – If a ball in motion is accidentally deflected or stopped by an outside agency, it is the rub of the green, no penalty is incurred and the ball shall be played as it lies except:
a: If a ball in motion after a stroke other than on the putting green comes to rest in or on any moving or animate outside agency, the player shall, through the green or in a hazard, drop the ball, or on the putting green place the ball as near as possible to the spot where the outside agency was when the ball came to rest in or on it, and ….

And it goes on like that for another few hundred words with notes and asterisks and subclauses and parenthetical remarks until the reader lapses into a coma. In fact, the Rules of Golf were originally written as a sleep aid before things like Ambien or the airing of "The Real Housewives of Greater Keokuk."

It's true.

But don't let that stop you from learning those rules and applying them in the correct situations. Learning the rules of golf can afford you a great deal of prestige among your playing partners. They will thank you for reminding them a ball hit out of bounds is subject to both stroke and distance penalties. They will applaud your astuteness when you assess them a two-stroke penalty for carrying an extra club in their bag. Heck, they will probably carry you off the course on their shoulders after you advise them that they have been disqualified from a tournament for signing an incorrect scorecard. Or they may bludgeon you with a gap wedge and bury you in a greenside bunker. It could go either way.

Because golf is played by a variety of players on a variety of different courses, situations are constantly cropping up that are not adequately covered under the Rules of Golf. When this occurs, it is up to the players and/or tournament director to deal with these individual situations. Thus, the Rules of Golf are constantly being updated, revised and interpreted. In the interest of providing you with the most up-to-date rule interpretations, here are a few land-mark decisions that have yet to be added to the Rules of Golf.

Rule 88-g – It is illegal to epoxy any portion of a competitor to his or her golf cart. This rule can be disregarded in the case of any player who insists on giving you a shot-by-shot review of his last six rounds.

Rule 911 – Should a player fail to turn his cell phone to silent upon beginning play and said phone goes off during another player's swing, the offending cell phone owner is subject to loss of hole and loss of phone. Nearby lakes, creeks and outhouses are all accept-able repositories for the offending phones.

Rule 7-11 – No shoes, no shirts, no service. Cashier cannot open safe.

Rule 007 – Excessive gadgetry is strictly prohibited. Laser-guided balls or clubs, radio-controlled golf carts and any club or ball with more than four syllables are banned. However, any device that can keep beer cold and is undetectable by a course marshal is always acceptable.

Rule 1776 – We the people, in order to form a more perfect union … sorry, wrong rule.

Rule 2-4-6-8 – No inane cheering on the course. Screaming "mashed potatoes," "Baba Booey," and the ever-popular "It's in the hole" every time a player clears the tee box will subject the perpe-trator to an hour of listening to Justin Bieber in a closed room.

Rule 1040 (Short Form) – Depreciate accruable income using schedule 3/DD43a for current fiscal year rather than schedule 3/DD43 as previously used for even-numbered years.

These are just a few of the rules that are soon to be added to the official rulebook, and I sincerely hope that they clear things up for you.

If you've learned nothing from this treatise–and I think it's safe to assume that you haven't–at least remember this: Golf is a game played by honorable people, and it is up to each individual golfer to maintain the integrity of the sport. So the next time you find yourself all alone, looking over an unplayable lie behind a copse of trees and your conscience is the only thing preventing you from employing your foot wedge to improve your lie by kicking that ball out to the fairway, keep this in mind: If you don't give that ball a good, healthy kick, it may not roll all the way to the short grass.

The Unwritten
Rules of Golf

The Unwritten Rules of Golf

GOLF IS ALL ABOUT RULES. THERE ARE RULES THAT GOVERN PRACTICALLY everything that could possibly arise on the course during a round of play. There are rules that cover how to mark your ball on the green, rules that cover lost balls, rules that cover in what order you should tee off. There are even rules that cover how and when you may clean your ball. And all these rules are written up in a little booklet called … *The Rules of Golf*.

Clever title, huh?

But as comprehensive as the official tome is, there are plenty of situations that are not covered in *The Rules of Golf*. Let's call these the *Unwritten Rules of Golf*. These are the items that, while not specifically addressed in the USGA's compendium of conduct, are universally known to be true. If you've played any amount of golf, you already know most of these, but for the sake of those just starting out, here are a few of the unwritten rules that you will most certainly learn for yourself the more you play.

MEN DRIVING CARTS

Men who are driving the cart are required to hang their left foot out of the cart while driving. I've seen women who do this too, but not many. The trait is somehow related to the Y chromosome and is believed to aid in steering.

MARSHALLS

Marshals will appear only when your group has lost three balls on one hole and your group has fallen behind by half a hole for the first time all day. Conversely, they will be nowhere to be found when you are following a group of golfers who treat every putt as if it is for a share of the lead of the U.S. Open and hunt for each lost ball with the kind of dedication normally reserved for independent diamond miners.

SCORING

Any time your opponent makes an "honest mistake" in scoring, the mistaken total will always result in him carding a score lower than that actually played.

BEVERAGE CARTS

The number of beverage carts on the course will be in inverse proportion to the temperature and stocked accordingly. Thus, when the temperature is below 45 degrees and the wind is howling, at least six carts will be assigned to each nine holes. They will have cold beer and pop as well as other iced beverages, but under no circumstances will they carry coffee or hot chocolate. As the temperature rises, beverage carts will be pulled from the course until only a single cart remains. This cart will be stationed no more than 100 yards from the clubhouse.

BEST SHOT EVER

The only time you will pure a 3-wood from the fairway will come on the heels of uttering the phrase, "I can't get there from here." It will be followed by a player in the group in front of you falling to his knees and grabbing either his head or his groin.

NOTE: The likelihood of this occurring goes up exponentially depending on the size and temperament of the group in front of you.

Thus, if you are playing behind a group of drunken, steroid-steep 300-pound former professional wrestlers, your chances of hitting a member of that foursome are better than having your dinner interrupted by a telemarketer.

THE PRACTICE GREEN

Under no circumstances will the practice putting green bear any resemblance to the greens on the actual course. If, by any chance, the practice green does have features even vaguely similar to those that may be encountered on the course, the practice green shall be mowed in such a way as to be either much faster or much slower than any other green to be found on that particular course.

LOST BALLS

The only lost ball you will ever find will be recovered only *after* you have dropped a replacement ball and hit it into a lake without declaring it provisional. When you do find that original ball, it will have somehow made its way to the middle of the fairway and be sitting up on a tee left over from yesterday's scramble.

HOLE IN ONE

A hole in one can be recorded only on the day you are on the verge of bankruptcy and you are playing in a tournament with 128 of your closest friends, every one of whom drinks only 12-year-old scotch.

GIVE AND TAKE

Three-hundred-yard tee shots will always be followed by thinned sand wedges that rocket past the green into a neighboring yard or parking lot.

HINDSIGHT

Your best round of the year will come on the one day you opted out of your normal $20 Nassau with automatic two-down presses.

BAD SHOTS

Your opponent's sliced ball will always bounce off a house and back into the fairway. Yours will break the $1,700 triple-paned window where the lawyer who owns the house is testing his new video camera.

BAD OMENS

Striping the ball and rattling pins on the range is the most certain of all precursors to chunked, thinned and pulled shots once you move to the first tee.

NO CAKE FOR YOU

The day you finally cure your yips on the putting green and begin dropping everything from inside 40 feet will be the same day you begin spraying your irons into adjacent fairways, parking lots and counties.

RETURN POLICY

The new driver you took out on the course to demo and with which you could do no wrong will become a tool of Satan the second your check clears the bank.

WEATHER REPORT

Your rain suit will be hanging up at home, freshly laundered, the day the skies open up and you are the greatest possible distance from the clubhouse. Your sunscreen will run out the day the temperature reaches 100 and there isn't a cloud in the sky.

AND NOW FOR SOMETHING COMPLETELY DIFFERENT

The lessons you finally break down and take will immediately cure your slight fade … and leave you with a vicious snap hook that you will live with the rest of your life.

This is hardly a definitive version of the Unwritten Rules of Golf. There are dozens of others that haven't been included, but don't worry. You'll discover them for yourself.

The Charity Event

The Charity Event

NOT EVERYONE PLAYS GOLF FOR FUN. FOR SOME, IT IS AN OBLIGATION. It is something they endure, usually once a year at the charity golf event in which they are obligated, for one reason or another, to participate.

It can be a stressful occasion, particularly for someone who doesn't play on a regular basis, but it doesn't have to be.

Here are some things you should know about these events that will help you get through them with minimal brain damage.

The first thing you need to remember is that this is going to be a long day.

Start drinking early.

With a normal round of golf, you show up to the course, whack a few balls on the range, and go play 18 holes. Maybe you stop off at the clubhouse afterward, but that's really up to you.

Not so at the charity golf tournament.

A typical charity golf tournament starts early in the morning. You need to get there in time to register, pay your fees and then run the gauntlet of additional extras, all of which benefit the noble cause you are there to support. Whether it's to aid the three-toed marmot habitat or raise funds to send an interpretive dance troupe to parts far away (how they get back is up to them), the organizers of the event will have put a ton of creativity into this event, and the least you can do is toss them a few bucks.

There are raffle tickets and mulligans available for purchase. Some tournaments offer bits of string you can buy to lessen the distance of putts you need to make. Still others have a variety of contests you can enter, like Longest Putt or Most Accurate Sand Shot or Just Give Us Your Wallet and We'll Tell You How Much We Need.

Don't worry about it. Try to remember you're there for the kids … or the dogs … or the local marching band. It doesn't matter. What matters is how you're going to make next month's house payment after financing a new wing for the pot-bellied pig spay and neuter clinic.

But you can worry about that later.

Now that you've lightened your wallet sufficiently, head over to the breakfast buffet and grab a couple mini-muffins.

Don't eat them!

They are not for human consumption. Stick them in your bag. They will come in handy later if you run out of balls.

Grab another drink. You haven't begun to have fun yet.

After hitting a few balls at the range and putting a few balls on the practice range, it's time for the tournament to get underway.

The format for the charity golf event is inevitably the scramble. The rules are simple: All four players on the team tee off, and then the best shot is selected. The entire team then plays their second shot from that spot. Once again the best shot is selected, and the entire team plays from there. The process is repeated until the team's ball is holed out and a team score is recorded.

This format allows inexperienced players to participate even if they play horribly, as they will be propped up by the better players on their team. It also allows those better players to test their patience as they try not to strangle those with whom they are paired.

Don't worry about any of that. The most important thing to remember is that this is a charity event, so don't get all caught up in winning … you're not going to. Somewhere in the host of golfers who will be playing that day is a team that was assembled with the singular goal of winning just this type of event. Each player on the team serves a very particular and vital role critical to the success of this tournament juggernaut.

The team is usually made up of one player who can stripe the ball 350 yards down the middle of any fairway, another who hits irons to greens like he is tossing coins into a wishing well, another who does nothing but putt and drops more six-footers than a discount undertaker. The fourth is there for his creative accounting which is rivaled only by Bernie Madoff.

This team travels the country playing in this type of event day in and day out, winning thousands of dollars in pro shop gift certificates that they then sell on the black market for pennies on the dollar. I don't understand the economics of it either. It's like a pyramid scheme or trickle-down economics–better not to question it and just move along.

Even though you have virtually no chance of winning this tournament, take heart. There will be beverage carts on the course, more welcome than an oasis in the Sahara, and you should avail yourself of them every chance you get. Have I mentioned it's going to be a long day?

Drink up.

After 18 holes of golf that shouldn't take more than six or seven hours, you are done with your round … and possibly the game of golf.

It's now time for what we'll call "lunch," for lack of a better word. It might be a taco bar prepared by people who have obviously never eaten a taco, or it could be hamburgers crafted from the same (oh, let's call it) meat from which the tacos were made. They are essentially interchangeable in that either can be just as easily tossed in the trash while no one is watching.

While enjoying your post-tournament meal, you'll have the chance to buy more raffle tickets and if you're lucky, bid on silent auction items, typically including everything from the tournament organizer's daughter's handmade golf ball holder made from real popsicle sticks and artificial macaroni to a trip for four to Pebble Beach.

Don't bid on that one.

You've been drinking and might have to live out of doors for a few months to fulfill your pledge.

There will also be sporting event tickets, memorabilia and other things you might not expect to find outside one of your pricier garage sales. And yes, I know. You already spent all your money earlier. Don't worry. They take credit cards, and there's an ATM in the pro shop just in case your bankcard hasn't already burst into flames.

By the end of the day your little golf outing will set you back just slightly more than the cost of a used Honda Accord or a three-day junket to Cancun.

But keep in mind, it's for a good cause.

After all, the heartbreak of psoriasis isn't going to cure itself.

And now it's time to go home. All that's left is to thank your host, collect (and pay for) the driver cover that looks like Sponge Bob Square Pants you won in the silent auction (it seemed like a good idea at the time) and try to find your car. On second thought, call a cab. You've been drinking all day. What were you thinking?

Teaching Your Wife to Golf

Teaching Your Wife to Golf

I HAVE BEEN MARRIED FOR MORE THAN **30** YEARS, AND IT IS NOT uncommon for people to ask me if there is a secret to a long marriage. Sometimes I tell them the secret is communication–being able to listen to your spouse and try to see things from his or her point of view. Other times I say it's all about compromise and trying to find common ground between two partners. And still other times I simply say, "Why are you in the men's room? You're not supposed to be in here."

The truth is, I don't know the secret to a long marriage, but I do know one way to ensure you will not have a long marriage: Try to teach your significant other to golf. Serial adultery is more easily forgiven.

But it goes on all the time.

Usually it happens at a "fun" couples golf outing where more than half the wives have been baited into playing their only nine holes of the year with the promise that it's "just for fun" and "there will be lots of others there who don't play" and "nobody takes this seriously."

Then, upon arrival, the unsuspecting spouse is ushered to the driving range, where her husband directs shot after shot with all the playfulness of a Yugoslavian gymnastics coach, squeezing every ounce of joy out of what could be a pleasant afternoon and establishing legal grounds for imminent divorce proceedings.

And it only gets worse out on the course.

With a whopping $10 prize on the line, husbands are transformed into field marshals, compelled to secure a victory by any means possible, rigidly imparting every golf tip they have ever heard and unsuccessfully employed to their poor mate just moments before she attempts to swing.

It usually goes something like this:

- Keep your head still.
- Rotate your shoulders.
- Keep your left arm straight.
- Shift your weight to your back foot.
- Bend your knee.
- Cock your wrists.
- Fire with your left leg.
- Keep your swing path on line.
- Shift your weight forward.
- Come through the ball hands first.
- Finish with your belt buckle to the target.
- End in a reverse C position.
- Batten down the hatches.
- Only you can prevent forest fires.
- Remember the Alamo!

It's just too much.

And once the swing is completed and the ball mishit, the husband chimes in disappointedly, "You didn't keep your arm straight."

No, but she did when she laid that 7-iron to your scalp, didn't she, Harvey Pennick?

Even the pros will admit they can keep only one or two thoughts in their head during the course of the swing, and they practice hours on end every day. Expecting your bride to be able to master Ben

Hogan's "Five Lessons" from your 30-second dissertation is about as reasonable as expecting Barack Obama and Rush Limbaugh to team up on Dancing with the Stars.

I take a different approach with my wife, and while we haven't won any tournaments using this methodology, I have also not had beer thrown on me as she drives hastily away in a golf cart … well, not lately, anyway.

Here's what I do. I give her one single tip to use that day.

Just one.

I might tell her, "relax your grip on the club" or "keep your tempo nice and smooth" or "don't be so uptight; nobody will see us."

What's the point in loading her up with information like she's cramming for the bar exam? You're out there together. Have some fun, hit a few balls, enjoy a couple cocktails and seriously, no one's watching, come over here.

Do I expect it to make her a great golfer in one afternoon? Of course not.

Do I think that she might swing a little better by focusing on a single swing thought rather than trying to remember a dozen? Absolutely.

Am I just kidding myself about successfully luring her behind the trees for a little work on her grip? Hey, a guy can dream.

Besides, my wife doesn't really care that much about golf.

The fact is, she would rather look good on the course than play well. She might not be willing to go to the driving range to work on her short game, but she will spend hours the night before a tournament picking out the outfit that will complement the ball she plans to play. Because God forbid your hair scrunchy, socks and visor don't match that metallic blue ball you're going to be knocking into the creek.

And while we're on the subject of balls, I've got to give it up to the guy that invented those metallic-colored balls. They cost more than the most expensive balls played by the top pros in the world. Is it because they go longer or reduce spin or have better feel around the green?

No!

It is because they are "adorable," and my wife simply must have them. They have been elevated beyond the lowly role of golf equipment to the much more lofty designation of "golf accessory."

Well played, metallic golf ball inventor.

But back to the point.

Yes, my wife cares more about her wardrobe than dropping a six-foot putt, and yes, she spends three times what I do on golf balls that are half as good, and yes, she may always be relegated to the drop area after any forced carry of more than 25 yards, but you know what?

I don't care.

She still looks good in that designer golf ensemble, and every once in a while she actually will sneak behind the trees with me, so I am not about to let some game drive a wedge (a sand wedge, if you will) between me and that woman.

Because when it comes to playing golf with your wife, having fun should be your only goal. Unless she is as competitive as you, just go with the flow. Don't take it too seriously. You might even look for some insight in the words of renowned sports psychologist and consultant to some of the greatest golfers on the planet, Dr. Bob Rotella, who said, "Golf is about how well you accept, respond to, and score with your misses much more so than it is a game of your perfect shots."

And to that, I would add, "If you try to teach your wife golf, trust me, you will not be 'scoring with your missus.'"

Golf on TV

Golf on TV

THERE IS NOTHING QUITE LIKE IT. THE ROLLING EXPANSES OF VERDANT fairways, the nail-biting drama of the 12-foot double-breaker with half a million dollars on the line, the very real possibility that I will fall asleep at some point during the telecast.

Don't get me wrong; I love golf on TV, but there's something about it that draws me napward quicker than a plate of Thanksgiving turkey with Ambien gravy. It is a more certain producer of sleep than swilling a bottle of Nyquil while you retell me that story of that thing your cat did with the bottle cap.

It's not that I am less than captivated with the action on the links. I think it has more to do with the way golf is broadcast and viewed by spectators in attendance. It is so different from other sports broadcasts. Televised golf has a solemnity normally associated with the reading of a will or a Nora Jones concert.

The announcers talk in hushed whispers as though they are relating a particularly embarrassing transgression in the confessional or discreetly trying to interest passersby in black market contraband.

"Hey. Psssst. Buddy. You want some golf?"

"No man. I'm trying to quit."

Even the photographers are ninja-like in their endeavors. They are less stealthy when trying to photograph cheetahs on the savanna than they are when trying to document a golf tournament.

And apparently those who are allowed to attend golf tournaments (with the notable exception of the Phoenix Open–those guys know how to party) are rigorously screened with the fervor of a disgruntled TSA worker. Of course, this has to be done in order to weed out the rowdies, loudmouths and anyone with a working larynx. Any talk uttered louder than a muffled whisper at a golf tournament is about as welcome as a hooker at an Amish quilting bee.

Surgical theaters have more boisterous hecklers, for crying out loud.

And those who break the silence are forcibly removed, their cardboard periscopes crushed and their lanyards ripped unceremoniously from their necks as they are ushered from the hallowed grounds.

While these procedures ensure the competitors won't be inconvenienced by such distractions as patrons unwrapping a snack or the deafening clamor of a camera shutter or a butterfly noisily landing on a flower petal, they also turn the course into the equivalent of a mausoleum.

Hell, babies' nap rooms have more built-in distractions.

In no other sport do we so tenderly coddle the athletes who are competing. Hockey has fist fights, football has the wave and international soccer fans aren't even allowed to purchase tickets unless they show proof of at least two felony convictions. Good Lord, library patrons are rowdier than golf spectators.

And the quiet exhibited at professional golf tournaments certainly bears no resemblance to the atmosphere surrounding the matches we amateurs play. They have thousands of people there watching them play, yet the gallery remains deathly still.

In contrast, teeing it up with my foursome is like stepping into the middle of a particularly animated Jerry Springer show. There are people yelling at each other, name calling, accusations flying. It's what I imagine Thanksgiving dinner to be like at the Lohan household.

Welcome to the Thunderdome!

The complete lack of respect shown to others in the group is in direct proportion to how much cash is on the line and how big an edge there is in the match. Show me a guy who's two down with three to play and 20 bucks on the line, and I'll show you a trash-talking, change-jangling, Velcro-ripping opponent who would have no qualms whatsoever spraying a little WD-40 on his opponent's grips should he be so foolish as to turn his back.

Face it, pro golfers are pampered like purse dogs on Rodeo Drive. It's time we quit treating professional golfers like bomb technicians. These guys are not transplanting organs; they are playing a game, so why not add a little excitement to the whole spectacle?

And here's how we do it.

Let's start by making it more like the game we play. How about encouraging competitors to engage in a little good-natured gamesmanship? Who wouldn't love to see a spray of flowers delivered to Tiger Woods on the #1 tee with a card that said only, "Miss waking up next to you," but with no name. He'd spend the rest of the tournament trying to figure out who they were from. And if for even a second you are thinking that's too mean, you are part of the problem in persistently pampering the pros.[10]

But I digress.

A player could hire a caddy who could also play the trombone and have him make that "WaaWaaWaaWaaWaa" trill of disappointment every time an opponent left a lag putt short.

---

10 I think Persistently Pampering the Pros is actually the name of a spa at Pebble Beach.

Hilarious.

And if we really want to make it similar to our game, let's take the next logical step. You've heard of "Beer Pong?" How about "Gimmee Guzzle?" If a pro misses a putt from inside 8 feet, he takes a shot. Make his caddy take two. It'll give new meaning to the terms "tight lie" and "in his bag."

Next, the "Buzzer Beater."

Here's how it works: When a player's turn comes up, he will have 30 seconds to strike the ball. If he fails to do so, the device will begin to make noise–something annoying, but bearable, like a tape of Dick Vitale commenting endlessly on the latest basketball phenom or the sound of a bug zapper laboring mightily on a June evening in Iowa.

If another 10 seconds pass and the shot remains untaken, we up the ante. Maybe a recording of Fergie singing about her "lovely lady lumps."

If that doesn't spur the chronologically-challenged golfer to action, all the stops should be pulled out and we get the sound of car alarms going off or a chain saw in full voice or a continuously looping tape of Fran Drescher laughing.

I know it sounds cruel, but sometimes you have to exhibit a little tough love. Employ this device at a couple of tournaments, and the excitement level will skyrocket while average playing times will plummet like a paralyzed osprey.

It's a win/win.

How about "Green Girls," a la the ring girls at boxing matches? Let's see how unflappable these paragons of professionalism really are when the person tending the flag is garbed in a bikini, spike heels and not much more. I can hear her giving him advice as he tries to concentrate on the putt.

"It looks like it breaks a little to the left."

"No. That's just the way my slacks are cut."

At the press conference following the match, the phrase "I was pulling my putts all day" will take on a whole new meaning.

Anyway, that's just a few ideas I had. I'm sure you have some great ones too. How about t-shirt cannons pumping out golf shirts to the gallery. Maybe in between shots, players should have to make balloon animals for their fans or engage in a quick round of charades.

Whatever it takes is fine, but let's breathe some life into the telecasts and make them a fun experience. Otherwise, you might as well be watching soccer.

The Comic Next Door

Award-winning speaker and comic Bob Meddles is available for public and private events both corporate and club.

And if you are looking to make your next golf event extra special, ask about the golf show.

For more information e-mail slaphappyent@gmail.com

or visit his website at www.BobMeddles.com.